MARILYN MONROE
FROM BEGINNING TO END

"Being with her people want not to die." — *Arthur Miller*

MARILYN MONROE
FROM BEGINNING TO END

NEWLY DISCOVERED PHOTOGRAPHS BY EARL LEAF

FROM THE MICHAEL OCHS ARCHIVES

TEXT BY MICHAEL VENTURA

BLANDFORD

"I'm so many people. Sometimes I wish I was just me." — Marilyn

CONTENTS

"I don't think I've ever met a writer I'd like as my judge."

— Marilyn Monroe

For Jo Carol Pierce

Blandford Press
An Imprint of the Cassell Group
Wellington House, 125 Strand, London WC2R 0BB

Text © Michael Ventura, 1997
Photographs © 1997 Michael Ochs Archives Ltd

British Library Cataloguing-in-Publication Data:
a catalogue record for this book is available from the British Library

ISBN 0-7137-2686-5

Designed and edited by DAG Publications Ltd. Designed by David Gibbons; edited by John Gilbert; printed and bound in Great Britain.

INTRODUCTION
by Michael Ochs

Over twenty years ago a friend informed me that Earl Leaf, a famous *paparazzo* photographer of the Fifties and Sixties, was dying of emphysema and he thought I should try to preserve his photographic work. I dutifully went to visit Leaf at his Hollywood home where he told me that he had already willed the negatives of his work to the teen magazines he had shot them for, so there was nothing I could do with his work.

Earl died in 1980 and, a little over a decade later, I found out that the teen mags Earl had sold his work to were going bankrupt and were selling their photo archive. I purchased their entire collection but found there were no Earl Leaf negatives there, only proof sheets. The publishers swore that they had never had the negs and that Earl had told them just to make prints off the proof sheets as that was good enough for magazine usage. Since they were apparently all that was left of Earl's work, I decided to file the proofs in the hope that I too could sometime take prints off the proofs.

While filing the Monroe proof sheets I noticed that some of them did not have Earl Leaf's name stamped on the back but read 'John R.' with an address in Yonkers, New York. I immediately called the man to ask if he knew where the Leaf negatives were. He replied that he had them and that Earl had willed them to him. It seemed, therefore, that Earl had misled me and left the negatives to John R., his photo processor, in exchange for free prints for the rest of his life.

I asked John R. what he had been doing with the negs for the last decade, to which he responded that he had just finished getting them in order but had done nothing with them. To the question of whether he was interested in selling them he replied that he 'had not really thought about it,' so I urged that he should think about it fast as I was on the plane.

I soon made the deal with John R. and purchased over 100,000 Earl Leaf negatives covering the entertainment world from the 1950s through to the 1970s. One of the unique parts of the collection was his coverage of Marilyn Monroe, from her earliest days in Hollywood until her untimely end. These newly uncovered and relatively unpublished photographs of Marilyn mark the first book from the works of Earl Leaf.

The search ends, the enjoyment begins.

MICHAEL OCHS, LOS ANGELES, 1997

THE WONDER AND THE CAMERAMAN

"I'm close, I can feel it, I can hear it, but it isn't really me."

— Marilyn Monroe, of her image

Marilyn Monroe. She first stepped before the cameras half a century ago and died more than thirty years ago, but we keep her close, we invoke her presence, we haven't let her go, and we won't let her rest. Because she doesn't let us rest. We keep thinking about her, writing and reading about her, as though somehow if we could understand her we might understand ourselves.

It's likely that at every moment in the day she's being watched somewhere in the world, in theaters and on televisions, subtitled or dubbed. (Imagine what Marilyn sounds like in Iraq, in Japan, in Kenya.) Of what other star could that be said with surety? Prostitutes in Bangkok, Mexican singers, American truck-stop waitresses, and trans- vestites the world over, still try to look like her. As with Elvis, imitating Marilyn has become a profession. And her photograph is everywhere, from the Warhol in New York's Museum of Modern Art to the magazine pages that paper the walls of the shanty-towns of Lima and Calcutta. Her affairs with Jack and Bobby Kennedy have forced even academic political scholars to consider her in their histories. No other woman of our century has had such a pervasive, inescapable impact.

Yet, at the center of that impact, there's a vacancy — a hole down which our attention pours, and which our attention can never fill. Billy Wilder, the director of *The Seven Year Itch* and *Some Like It Hot*, said, "She never flattens out on the screen. In any scene she is in, there is never what I call a hole in the screen. She never gets lost up there. You can't take your eyes away from her. You can't watch any other performer when she's playing a scene with somebody else." Yet there *is* a hole in — what can we call it? — her significance. She *did* get lost up there. She was never sure of, she was desperately uncertain about, what she meant to herself; and we have never been sure of what she's meant to us.

Somewhere between our eye and her image, her uncertainty meets ours. In that shared uncertainty is our mutual compulsion, hers to be seen and ours to see, and it opens us to a hundred, a thousand questions — questions about ourselves, about her, about the compulsions and the world that we share. It is the special grace of Marilyn Monroe that she endows those questions with an air of wonder.

"I like animals. If you talk to a dog or a cat it doesn't tell you to shut up." — Marilyn

"When you're a failure in Hollywood — that's like starving to death outside a banquet hall with the smells of filet mignon driving you crazy."

— Marilyn Monroe

If Earl Leaf was famous for anything, it was for getting along with the famous. Gadding around Asia as a photo-journalist in the 1930s, he managed to take that decade's only photograph of Mao Tse Tung. One can only guess at the combination of hustling, persistence, and charm, that it took to finagle such a meeting. Two decades later he dated Kim Novak — or at least accompanied her to several photo-ops. And once, probably in 1950 or 1951, at a C-list or even Z-list Hollywood party that was fizzling badly, Marilyn Monroe felt comfortable enough with him to say, "Let's blow this joint and go live it up somewhere."

Leaf declined her invitation. Maybe he had something more pressing to do; or maybe Leaf sensed hungers in Marilyn that he didn't want to touch, even casually; or maybe she just wasn't famous enough yet.

And *was* Marilyn comfortable with him? Or was it that she knew Earl was a fanzine photographer (they'd already shot their first session) and thought that since the party wasn't going anywhere it wouldn't

Marilyn to Earl Leaf: "Let's blow this joint and go live it up somewhere."

hurt to be nice to this gangly, smiling, weird-looking cat who could get her into the magazines? Her ravenous ambition during these years has been well-documented. And she herself said, "There was a period when I responded too much to flattery and slept around too much, thinking it could help my career, though I always liked the guy at the time. They were always so full of self-confidence and I had none at all and they made me feel better."

Did she always like the guy at the time? She certainly needed to convince herself she did. Still, Leaf was a singular man, and she might well have enjoyed his quirkiness. Someone who could charm Mao Tse Tung and his staff might well charm a young starlet. In their photos together she looks at ease, which is rare for her. But Marilyn could look any way she wanted to — "I can make my face do anything," she once said. So, as usual, we'll never know. In any case, Leaf later said often, and in fanzine print, that he regretted "turning down a date with Marilyn." No doubt by that time he did.

The end of World War Two found Earl Leaf in Los Angeles and in his heyday — which lasted from the late Forties to the early Sixties, the very years of Marilyn's career. This was when the movie fanzines were still going strong, and when a starlet in skimpy underwear was considered soft porn. The photos that only men's magazines would print then were

Leaf's all charm, but Marilyn seems unable to bear the sight of one more party-snack

often not as revealing as advertisements on billboards and in newspapers now, but they were certainly in demand. Earl Leaf made his living supplying that demand, and being one of the gaggle of *paparazzi* popping flashbulbs at any celebrity, at any photo-op, in a Hollywood adrift during the final days of the old studio system.

A professional *paparazzo.* That was Earl Leaf.

Leaf remained in Los Angeles until his death in 1980. He died leaving little behind but file cabinets stuffed with contact sheets, negs, silly old magazines, and a poorly written, unfinished autobiography — a work the aging Leaf no doubt dreamed might be a best-seller. After all, wasn't *he* important too? Hadn't he known Marilyn and Mao?

A Hollywood death if there ever was one, the *real* Hollywood: all those small apartments between Echo Park Boulevard and Doheny where thousands no one will ever hear of hang on forever, or what seems like forever, honing whatever talents they may or may not have, trying to beg, impress, work, cheat, fuck or luck their way into the big time. Until one day they're too spent, too old, or too dead.

Yet as it turns out, gangly weird star-gawking Earl left us something after all — for Earl Leaf's beatnik air of intelligence went deeper than a pose. When, years after Leaf's death, archivist Michael Ochs got hold of his photographs, he found that Leaf, while not a great artist, was a superb *paparazzo.*

The superstar and the paparazzo, united in trying (without much success) to look interested

It's not only that Leaf had mastered the difficult and under-rated craft of the photo-journalist, the ability to frame an interesting shot on the run, in the midst of confusion; it's how, in the middle of all that bustle, Leaf managed to make his shots strangely intimate. A considerable feat. Again and again his photographs of the stars reveal a face we have never quite seen before — a shade, an expression, a flicker, a gesture, a connection, a clue. Just one more clue in the unending mystery of stardom, yes, but no one can deny our hunger for such clues, for each clue. From semiotic academics writing tomes on cinema to Valley girls reading *People* as they get their hair done, there's a suspicion that if we can understand the stars, or at least our own relation to a specific star, we will be closer to the secret of ourselves. Leaf left us many a clue.

With Marilyn, we need every clue we can get. Looking at Leaf's first and last photos of Marilyn, many might not recognize that this is even the same woman. Which is why Leaf is especially valuable to the contemplation of her. No one else we know of photographed Marilyn Monroe over the entire span of her public life. None of her more well-known photographers knew her as early and recorded her across such a spectrum. Leaf photographed Monroe eight times from 1950 to 1962. His first shots were taken days before the release of her first significant pic-

"I think I have one talent: observing. I hope that it adds up to acting." — *Marilyn*

ture, *The Asphalt Jungle*; his last are undated, but were done no more than weeks before her death.

Studying Leaf's Monroe, searching for clues to this woman who means so much to us, yet whose meaning is so vague, the effect is like time-lapse photography. This book, then, is a series of biographical essays, meditations on the life of Marilyn Monroe through the clues left by Earl Leaf. There is one essay per photo-session, eight in all. The hoped-for effect is a composite, a montage, in which Marilyn becomes more real to us without losing her (and our) wonder.

"When you are famous every weakness is exaggerated." — *Marilyn*

"If I'd observed all the rules, I'd never have got anywhere." — *Marilyn*

1950

THE LAST OF THE SECRET YEARS

"I knew how third-rate I was. I could actually feel my lack
of talent, as if it were cheap clothes I was wearing inside.
But, my God, how I wanted to learn. To change, to
improve! I didn't want anything else. Not men, not
money, not love, but the ability to act."

— Marilyn Monroe

On the cloudy afternoon of May 17, 1950, Earl Leaf showed up in the
yard of a Beverly Hills mansion to photograph a no-name starlet. It was
just another gig. He shot a roll and started to pack up. "Poor kid," he
later said, "she thought I was going so soon because it was no good. She
pleaded with me to try a little longer. She said, 'I can climb trees, do
hand-stands, cartwheels — anything you like.' And for twenty minutes
she knocked herself out trying to give me original poses. I couldn't make
her see it was unnecessary."

She played with a dog, she bounced a ball, she hung from trees, arranged flowers, hosed the lawn. She changed clothes three times. And she *did* do cartwheels and hand-stands. She even read a script, and in two different outfits — obviously a pose she insisted on. That was her first attempt on record to ask the media and the studios to take her seriously.

This is very much the young woman Emmeline Snively described. Snively gave Marilyn her first modelling job at the Blue Book Agency in 1945. (Its offices were in the Ambassador Hotel, the same place where Marilyn's last love, Robert Kennedy, would be killed in 1968.) Snively said, "Girls ask me all the time how they can be like Marilyn Monroe. And I tell them, if they showed one tenth of the hard work and gumption that that girl had, they'd be on their way."

Does the woman in these photographs, two weeks from her twenty-fourth birthday, look like someone who had by then studied *The Human Fabric*, an authoritative work on anatomy by Andreas Vesalius? She marked the book "in detail," as biographer Graham McCann put it, "and even at the end of her life would still instruct young friends with an encyclopedic knowledge of the human bone structure."

Does she look like she'd studied make-up with such subtlety that even the master studio make-up craftspeople, the best in the world, would be in awe of her? Whitey Snyder, one of these masters, and the

"The greatest thing about Monroe is not her chest. It is her ear. She can read comedy better than anyone else in the world." — Billy Wilder, director

make-up man who prepared her corpse for the funeral, said: "Marilyn has make-up tricks that nobody else has and nobody knows."

Does she look like someone who preferred, all her (unmarried) life, to live alone, and who read incessantly, even desperately? Does she look like someone with a natural flair for language, using it always with freshness and originality?

Does she look torn between ambition and insecurity? Between knowing she was special and feeling she was worthless?

Does she look literally tortured by gynecological pains at their most extreme, a true "curse" (as they said in her generation), which had gripped her from her first periods? As McCann wrote, "No biography of Marilyn Monroe contains an adequate appreciation of the effect these illnesses had upon her outlook, her behavior (particularly her 'lateness'), or her own aspirations."

Does she even look like a sexpot? Or like someone who, at least in her youth, was said by her first husband and others to have an insatiable sexual appetite, and — what can I tastefully call it? — a commensurate sexual aptitude?

Does she look like someone of whom Arthur Miller said, with what turned out to be gruesome irony: "Being with her people want not to die." Does she look doomed? What, at this point, is the relationship between the woman and the camera?

"I dreamed of becoming so beautiful that people would turn and look at me when I passed." — *Marilyn*

Does she look like a woman of extraordinary secrets, even to this day? More books have been written on Marilyn Monroe than on any other Hollywood figure, yet only in 1988 did anyone know *what her first movie was.* All the biographies, all the reference books, said (many still say) it was *Scudda Hoo! Scudda Hay!* (1948), a silly piece of celluloid in which she's virtually an extra. Actually, she first appeared in 1947's *The Shocking Miss Pilgrim*, as a switchboard operator.

This isn't just a little mishap of scholarship. Its implications are large. The years 1945–50 are the least known of Marilyn's career. They are what Billy Wilder would call an enormous hole in the screen. This is the period in which she learned how to be photographed — the time when she worked incessantly on developing that incredible relationship between herself and the lens. This is when she taught herself the craft, not of performing, but of beauty. ("I dreamed of myself becoming so beautiful that people would turn and look at me when I passed.") This is when she worked incessantly to get into pictures. This is when she, in her phrase, "slept around" the most.

Her first screen role could have been no small thing to the recently renamed Norma Jeane (her spelling). Why did she never mention it? She was very concerned with honesty in her press releases. When she became important enough to get her way, she wouldn't allow the standard Hollywood ghost-written fanzine article, saying:

"Hollywood's a place where they'll pay you a thousand dollars for a kiss, and fifty cents for your soul." — Marilyn

"I might never see that article and it might be okayed by somebody in the studio. This is wrong because when I was a little girl I read signed stories in the fan magazines and I believed every word the stars said in them."

Nevertheless, for years she claimed to be an orphan, though her mother and father were still alive. And she never mentioned what must have been an enormous moment in her life, her first film role, *The Shocking Miss Pilgrim*. Her husbands didn't know about it. Historians didn't know. Intimate friends never knew.

She tried to conceal her childhood from the press because the fiction of being an orphan, painful as that might seem, was not as wounding as her mother's madness, her grandmother's psychotic attempt to kill her, and the physical and sexual abuse she suffered in several of the eleven foster homes (plus one orphanage) that were her life until her first marriage at age sixteen.

It is reasonable to assume that something she would conceal more completely than her childhood was, in her view, more wounding.

What was so painful about the experience of her first film that she never spoke of it to anyone we know of? We can't expect to find out, but it's worth mentioning that in spite of her rough childhood, people who knew Marilyn before 1947 don't describe the incredibly insecure, continu-

Earl Leaf cannot have known how similar this photo would be to one of Marilyn's most famous movie scenes

ally frightened, born-to-be-doomed woman that everyone speaks of from 1950 on. The biographer who did the most extensive and dependable research on her early years, Fred Lawrence Guiles, said, "The world outside was far more tempting to this little girl than to the other children [in the neighborhood]. Nothing daunted her." And her first husband, Jim Doughtery, spent half his life repeating to interviewers that his young wife Norma Jeane (they were divorced in 1945) was totally different, bore no resemblance, to the way everyone characterized Marilyn Monroe.

A hole in the screen, indeed. *Something* happened. Later Marilyn would talk frankly to the press about her childhood — more frankly, in fact, than any other star before or since — but she only referred to the years 1945–50 in the most general way. She'd say little more than that she took acting, singing, and dancing lessons tirelessly. Her silence couldn't have been because that period was uneventful. She was a sexy, ambitious young woman, getting as much modeling work as she could handle and trying to break into movies. That's not an uneventful life. These Earl Leaf photographs, then, are portraits of a woman trying both to hide and to expose herself.

This would be the central tension of Marilyn Monroe's life.

The girl Earl Leaf found in that yard in 1950 had by then been in six films that she admitted to. A month before, United Artists had released

"She communicated such a charge of vitality as altered our imagination of life."
— Diana Trilling, critic

the first in which she was noticed, the Marx Brothers' *Love Happy.* Two days after this photo session, Fox would release *A Ticket to Tomahawk* (in which no one was noticed). And three days after that, on May 23, MGM would debut the first picture that caused her name to be mentioned in a review, John Huston's *The Asphalt Jungle.*

It was a tough, uncompromising *noir* story. One reviewer said that the newcomer Marilyn Monroe "lent a documentary effect" to the "lurid exposition" of the film. They didn't think she was acting — though Marilyn would later consider *The Asphalt Jungle* her finest work. Perhaps she was familiar enough with the dark characters of the story to give her acting its natural, unposed air. In any case, the film debuted six days after Earl Leaf photographed her, and her life would never be the same. Within the next year, her small parts in *All About Eve*, *The Fireball*, *Hometown Story*, *As Young As You Feel*, *Love Nest*, and *Let's Make It Legal*, would bring in more fan-mail, *much* more fan-mail, than the studio's biggest stars. Which is why Marilyn Monroe could say with certainty, "If I am a star, the people made me a star. No studio, no person, but the people did."

The Beverly Hills backyard in these photos belonged to Johnny Hyde, the dying super-agent who shunned his family to take Marilyn for a mistress. He did everything he could for her, tried to protect her, certainly loved

*"I've given pure sex appeal very little thought. If I had to think about it,
I'm sure it would frighten me." — Marilyn*

her. When he knew he was dying, he offered to marry her. He was a millionaire. He wanted her to have it. She would have been fixed for life. She turned him down. Told him, "I do love you, but I'm not *in* love with you." Hyde asked friends to try to convince her to marry him. She told one that she couldn't because when Johnny Hyde touched her she felt "no buzz in the arm." She couldn't marry anybody who didn't make her feel that, not even a dying man who was marrying her only to protect her future — a future he clearly didn't have much confidence in.

That young woman is in some of Earl Leaf's shots. A kind of clarity and a distinctive integrity. Not "integrity" as some would define it — she'd sleep around, do work she didn't believe in, lie. Her integrity was to her own, secret emotional center, and to her own version of authenticity.

Johnny Hyde died in December of 1950. Does Earl Leaf's pin-up look like someone who would go to the funeral even though Hyde's family told her not to? Does she look like someone of whom Hyde's son would say, "All I can recall clearly is Marilyn screaming my father's name over and over again. It shook everyone."

Does she look like someone who, two weeks after that funeral, would attempt suicide (the first attempt anyone knows about)?

In later years Marilyn would hold almost nothing back from the camera. At this point in her life, she was holding back almost everything.

"She can make any move, any gesture, almost insufferably suggestive." — Henry Hathaway, director

Earl Leaf was at his best taking photographs in the midst of hubbub. His posed sessions are usually his least interesting. But Marilyn forced Leaf into doing more than he came for, and in a few shots it paid off. Especially the most natural shot (see page 37), standing straight, in front of the white fence, holding her dog on a leash, her arm extended in a gesture, perhaps while suggesting a new pose to Earl. Leaf had come to shoot a starlet, and Marilyn had offered him a starlet, but in this shot he caught the woman who had been and the woman who would be.

I can think of no other early photograph of Marilyn in which her intelligence is so evident. This is a face of experience and intent. There's more than a hint of darkness. Also, hardness. ("I didn't want anything else. Not men, not money, not love.") This is a face that would be difficult to fool. This is a woman who could say, as she later did, "I was never kept; I always kept myself."

How did a high-school drop-out, victim of eleven foster homes, learn the poise and posture we see in every photograph?

"A lot of people will tell you it's all publicity. That's malarkey. They've tried to give a hundred girls the same publicity build-up. It didn't take with them." — Joseph Cotton

*"I can climb trees, do handstands, cartwheels, anything you like!" —
Marilyn to Earl Leaf*

*By age 24, the transformation from Norma Jeane Baker to Marilyn Monroe
is complete*

1952
FIRST YEAR OF STARDOM

"The truth is I've never fooled anyone. I've let men sometimes fool themselves. Men sometimes didn't bother to
find out who and what I was. Instead they would invent a
character for me. I wouldn't argue with them. They were
obviously loving somebody I wasn't. When they found
this out, they would blame me for disillusioning them —
and fooling them."

— Marilyn Monroe

It is a different face. Just before Johnny Hyde's death in December of 1950
she'd had cosmetic surgery: her nose was softened some at the point, and
her jawline was accented ever so slightly. They were subtle, brilliant
choices, worthy of a woman who'd made her own study of bone structure.
It's not that this face is more beautiful than the other; it's simply a more
expressive instrument. Virtually any photograph comparing the two faces
is testament to that. It's now a face that could, as she put it, "do anything."

Marilyn Monroe knew the worth of her creation. "I want to grow old without face-lifts," she once said. "They take the life out of a face, the character. I want to have the courage to be loyal to the face I've made."

Not "the face I have," but "the face I've *made.*" She took full responsibility for it. She knew it was a face of character; and, because it was, she knew it would take courage to be loyal to that face. "Courage" and "loyal" are unusual words to apply to one's face. It's as though she felt that the unique beauty she'd created had become something she had to live up to — as though she had created that beauty *in order to live up to it.* Perhaps, voracious reader that she was, she'd come across a comment by her favorite historical figure, Abraham Lincoln: "After forty a man has the face he deserves." It may be a harsh way to judge oneself, but Marilyn accepted that challenge.

When beauty is a gift, it's both a blessing and burden. When beauty is a choice, it's a journey. The lost-little-girl, born-to-be-doomed, victimized character who's usually presented in biographies as Marilyn Monroe, doesn't jibe with the starlet and star who created her own look, perfected her gifts, embarked on her journey. What she found on that journey was many times more terrible than she'd anticipated, and it destroyed her. But being destroyed by the consequences of your own journey isn't the same as getting run over by somebody else's. Marilyn Monroe deserves to be remembered as much more than a victim.

"I want to have the courage to be loyal to the face I've made." — *Marilyn*

Paparazzi don't get private sessions with stars, and from 1952 Earl Leaf would be photographing Monroe only at Hollywood parties, press events, and film premières — for 1952 was Marilyn's first year of stardom. Not that you'd know this by looking at her filmography. In three of her five films that year, she received no better than fourth billing: below Barbara Stanwyck, Paul Douglas, and Robert Ryan, in *Clash By Night*; below Victor Moore, Jane Darwell, Fred Allen, and Ginger Rogers, in *We're Not Married*; and below Cary Grant, Ginger Rogers, and Charles Coburn in *Monkey Business.* Yet she pulled in many times more fanmail than all those stars put together.

The journalists covering these films weren't interested in her costars; they were only interested in Marilyn. No one has ever been more consistently on the covers of more magazines for as long a time. 1952 was the first year that Marilyn was everywhere. (There has yet to be a last.) In addition, she'd begun her affair with Joe DiMaggio, and nothing in America in 1952 was reported as thoroughly. With the exceptions of Charlie Chaplin and Greta Garbo, no Hollywood figure had ever become such a pervasive icon so quickly.

But even Chaplin and Garbo achieved their celebrity in groundbreaking pictures that featured Chaplin and Garbo. Marilyn was doing it through bit-parts and supporting roles. It was as Billy Wilder later said, "You can't watch any other performer when she's playing a scene

The dress and laugh say it all — still confined to secondary roles, she was intent on making an impression, and she knew how

with somebody else." Something about her mesmerized America. It didn't seem to matter what sort of film she was in. Getting second billing to Richard Widmark in 1952's *Don't Bother to Knock*, she plays a babysitter who goes psychotic and terrorizes children. It was her first real acting task, and the role certainly clashed with her already pervasive public image. Nobody seemed to notice. Next year she played a murderess in *Niagara*, the first picture in which she received top billing. The public didn't care what she played. Even this early in her career, they feasted on her extraordinary presence; neither her psychosis in *Don't Bother to Knock* nor her mercilessness in *Niagara* (both played convincingly), could interrupt or distract from the public's visual feast.

It's not surprising that she was beginning to be overwhelmed; already her journey was taking her into a territory with no signposts and no boundaries. No one had ever been there before.

The poetic explanation for her appeal — an explanation that the artistic community seems to have agreed on — was put best by her third husband Arthur Miller: "Her beauty shines because the spirit is forever showing itself." But she didn't let much that was lyrical, or even gentle, shine through her persona in 1952 and 1953, the years that clinched her super-stardom. What was forever showing itself in those years was her body.

Has the camera caught her in a blink, or is she bored?

But many actresses were willing to display their bodies. What made Marilyn's display so compelling? I think it was this: the abandon with which she offered her body for view seemed genuine and often joyful. Even in *The Misfits*, her last film, when she is clearly so troubled, her display of her body is still so generous. Sensual actresses — from Jean

Harlow to Rita Hayworth to Ava Gardner — had always displayed themselves in a kind of defiant sulk (as Madonna does now). Their tough
poses said: "I know a lot of people think it's wrong for a woman to look
this sexy, but I'm going to brazen it out." The tougher they looked, the
more they seemed haunted by guilt, and the more they played to the
guilt in their audience.

Marilyn loved the camera too much for guilt to enter into that
special, star-to-lens relationship. She displayed herself with abandon,
and with every evidence of joy — as though it was the only fun she ever
really had. (From what we know of her, this may well have been true.)

Toward the end she would say, "I want to be an artist, not an
erotic freak. I don't want to be sold to the public as a celluloid aphro-
disical. Look at me and start shaking." She was too honest to leave the
statement there, however. She finished by saying: "It was all right for the
first few years. But now it's different."

Yet in spite of many statements like this, and no matter how haggard she later became, she never resisted the temptation to display her sexuality before a camera, and she never did it with anything but a sense of
fun. Three months before her death, when she was barely holding herself
together, she showed up on the set (a rare occurrence by then) for the now-
famous swimming-pool scene. She was supposed to wear a body-stocking.
She wouldn't. No major star had ever been shot naked in a studio film; she

He doesn't exactly seem her type, but the frank ambition in her expression lets us know exactly what the stakes are

knew she was breaking every rule. Yet in front of cast and crew she cavorted naked in the pool, with a heartbreaking look of fragility and delight.

It was what she'd always wanted to do. Other sensual stars gave the impression that they were *about* to take off their clothes — if we'd only be patient. But Marilyn acted as though she was way ahead of us. From the first, even in her bit-parts, she gave the impression that she was already naked.

It was a look she carefully and painstakingly intended. It's not enough to blame her sexy fame on the studios. The studios were responsible for her early film roles, but they weren't responsible for how she appeared, and behaved, in public. There is plenty of testimony that Marilyn worked for hours before going out to achieve her "party" look — a look that made her seem naked even though she had clothes on.

When asking why she chose to make this impression, we need to go beyond theories and jargons and remember that Marilyn Monroe loved to be naked. She walked around naked much of the time wherever she lived, and, in the early years, wherever she worked. Her acting coach Natasha Lytess remembered that she "ambled unconcerned, completely naked, around her [studio] bungalow, among wardrobe women, make-up girls, hairdressers. Being naked seems to soothe her — almost hypnotize her."

As a child she day-dreamed about being naked in church: that everyone would fall asleep while, naked, she stepped among them

"Anything's possible, almost." — Marilyn

"without hurting anybody." Nakedness was an intoxication for her, somehow holy (the fantasy was in a church). She dreamed that it would both make her powerful and harmlessly disarm others. Nakedness was, for Marilyn, a dream-like state both invoked and intensified by the presence of a camera. This was so much a part of her that she conveyed the sense of being naked on film no matter what she wore. The coda, perhaps the epitaph, to her life as a performer, was that her last studio footage finally recorded her nakedness without artifice — and that this was her choice.

We talk a lot about sex. We usually lie. And even when we speak honestly, what we say, no matter how erudite, is usually beside the point. But no one can deny that as a civilization we're obsessed with sex, and that sometimes sex can save or wreck a life. But what about sex as fun? *Really* fun? The pretense goes on everywhere (including the bedroom), but the reality is rare in anybody's life. It was rare in Marilyn's. But not when she was in front of a camera. And this, finally, is what people found irresistible.

This is also why she was (and remains) popular with women as much as with men. Her sensuality photographed so powerfully that it provoked the sensuality of her audience, regardless of gender. Undefined possibilities of abandonment and joy radiated from her.

"Sometimes I'm invited places to kind of brighten up a dinner table. You're just an ornament." — Marilyn

So it's not enough to say that she was sexy; and it's a dodge to blame her image on others. With considerable discipline she created her look, and portrayed sexuality on a level of pure, abandoned fun that most people would feel guilty, frightened, and insecure even to imagine. We watched Marilyn imagine for us. And then we imagined her.

"All we demanded was our right to twinkle." — Marilyn, of herself and
her fellow stars

1953
THE SUPER-STAR

"Being a movie actress was never as much fun as dreaming
of being one."

— Marilyn Monroe

His wife on his arm or not, Bogart couldn't help looking down Marilyn's
dress. Neither could the rest of America.

A friend of mine, Ramsey Wiggins, said once of some friends of
his: "They got what they wanted and it cost them everything they
needed." It's a sentence I think of often, contemplating Marilyn Monroe.
Earl Leaf took these shots a year and a half after his last Monroe images.
They show a very different woman on a very different night — November 4, 1953, the première of *How to Marry a Millionaire*, starring Betty
Grable, Lauren Bacall, and Marilyn. It was a night that confirmed Marilyn's achievement of everything she had ever wanted — a night when
what she needed still seemed almost in reach.

January of 1953 saw the release of *Niagara*, a film few watch
now. It broke records then, because it was Marilyn's first starring role.

With July came *Gentlemen Prefer Blondes*, featuring the flawless direction of Howard Hawks, the best song-and-dance Marilyn ever did ("Diamonds Are a Girl's Best Friend"), and the marvelous rapport between Marilyn and co-star Jane Russell. It stands with *Some Like It Hot* and *The Misfits* among the Monroe films that feel as vivid and present now as then. November's *How to Marry a Millionaire* has dated badly, but it was an enormous hit in its day, and much bally-hooed as the second movie ever shot in Cinemascope (the first was a religious epic, *The Robe*).

Cinemascope had been intended for spectacles, not for situation comedies, but Marilyn's body was deemed spectacle enough for Hollywood's second hype of the wide screen. We take that screen for granted now, but then it was a sensation. Of Marilyn's effect one critic wrote, "If you insisted on sitting in the front row, you would probably feel like you were being smothered in baked Alaska."

Even without a big screen, seeing her in these photographs creates a similar impression — which is no accident, but a Marilyn Monroe creation. Bogie and Bacall are under the same lighting as Marilyn, with the same flashbulbs popping at them, but Marilyn photographs brighter than they. She reflects more light. Not only has she selected her gown for this effect, but she's used her extraordinary mastery of make-up so that her flesh — arms and torso, as well as face — are reflectors too. (The hours it took to achieve this explain some of her legendary

Many friends testify that Marilyn was most at ease around children

lateness.) In fact, she reflects so much that people who get close enough (a girl looking over her shoulder, a boy she hugs) pick up some of Marilyn's shine. She looks like she's just stepped off a movie screen without losing its special gleam, and, goddess-like, can dispense that magic to whom she pleases. Everybody noticed this, even the reviewers. As one pointed out, "Miss Monroe looks as though she would glow in the dark."

Bogie and Bacall seem like regular people, hardly stars, next to Marilyn. Pause at that a moment: consider how difficult it was to achieve; the ambition necessary even to try; the need at the core of such ambition; and, finally, her ambition's victory. Bacall is twenty-nine, Monroe is twenty-seven, but they look like women of different generations. Or rather, Marilyn Monroe has achieved a "timeless twenties" look, as though she was born and will ever remain the age she is this night; while Lauren Bacall, standing beside her, looks ten years more than her true age and, like all mortals, destined to decay. In fact everyone seems fragile and mortal beside Marilyn this night, even children. It is as though they're being visited by an immortal, a goddess.

Marilyn, then, seems utterly unreal, yet without seeming false. It seems rather that reality can't touch her. So she achieved a look that reflected both her own deepest dream and the dreams of so many others.

Reviewing *The River of No Return*, the following year, Archer Winston of the *New York Post* wrote well of Monroe's attraction: "There is

Marilyn rarely laughed in films, yet in some photos we can almost hear it

something at once incongruous and strangely stimulating in Miss Monroe's dazzled and dazzling [appearance]. She herself is a leading representative of the natural instinct mentioned previously [sex], but she is also, by reason of the artificial aspect of her coloring and make-up, in opposition to nature. This creates a kind of tension, not too easily defined, but very easily translated into publicity, popularity, and public interest."

It was as though everyone was saying, "We can't believe you — but we *do* believe you!" As though we watched a magician of such impressive dexterity that we stopped believing in dexterity, and believed instead in magic.

Already the actual day-to-day work of movie-making was Marilyn's hell. Lauren Bacall remembered, "She would say to me, 'Let's talk. There's nobody I can talk to.' She wanted someone... I liked her, but not because I could have any real exchange with her. I think she was confused... We would be waiting around – eleven o'clock, and no Marilyn... She was always late, but I think it was in terror. She couldn't face what she was called upon to do; she couldn't cope."

One of her make-up men, Allan Snyder, agreed that Marilyn felt "terror, pure terror," toward acting. More than three years later, while Monroe was shooting *The Prince and the Showgirl*, Irina Baranova told

"Somehow I feel they know that I mean what I do. I always do mean 'Hello' and 'How are you?'" — *Marilyn*

director Laurence Olivier, "She has a quite unconscious but basic resistance to acting. She loves to show herself ... but to be an actress is something she does not want at all."

This may be the closest anyone has come to deciphering Marilyn's hysterical dread during virtually any film production. There is no doubt that Marilyn wanted desperately to be an actress; but there is also a lot to indicate that she wanted to be an actress in order to prove herself. Needing to prove yourself is not at all the same as needing to express yourself.

She didn't trust her fundamental genius, which was to be photographed. The literati she respected so much, and from whom she took her cues, didn't recognize being photographed as an art, and would never concede that a model could be an artist on the level of, say, an actress or a playwright. Marilyn desired desperately to push her way beyond the frame of the still camera and into the world of the moving picture, to go from the illegitimacy of one art to the legitimacy of another. But in motion pictures an actor cannot control what is revealed — not only because there are writers, directors, producers, and other actors exerting so many influences, but because motion pictures don't stop. Identity isn't fragmented frame by frame in motion pictures; identity is discovered by the camera in one state, and then must move (while keeping its consistency) into other states, with no let-up. For

"Pretty is just how good you apply your base." — Jayne Mansfield, who fashioned her image on this particular look of Marilyn's

someone who felt as insignificant and fragile in her core identity as Marilyn Monroe, the strain was unbearable. It was difficult enough for her to keep hold of her own identity; it was literally maddening to broaden that identity into an acted performance.

On the set of *Some Like It Hot* five years later, someone found a note she'd written to herself: "What am I so afraid of? Why I am I so afraid? Do I think I can't act? I know I can act but I am afraid. I am afraid and I should not be and I must not be." Marilyn couldn't bear this fear all alone. Throughout her career she depended heavily on her acting coaches, teachers, and therapists. Too heavily, many thought. "There were a lot of leeches in her life," Lauren Bacall said. "She made a lot of blunders in accepting the wrong people." From 1948 until she began attending Lee Strasberg's Actor's Studio in New York in the late 1950s, Marilyn's coach was Natasha Lytess — a woman considered strange even in Hollywood. (Lytess once said, "Marilyn needs me like a dead man needs a coffin.") Bacall remembered, "She would look past the director towards the coach. She often didn't seem to see anyone else, she would look past them or through them." The takes Lytess approved of were the takes that were used. When confronted about this by an interviewer, Marilyn answered: "I'm nobody's slave and never have been. Nobody hypnotizes me to do this or that... I didn't get help from [my directors]. I had to find it elsewhere."

Some directors hated Marilyn's coaches, and sometimes barred them from the set; other directors didn't mind. Otto Preminger (*River of No Return*) and Laurence Olivier (*The Prince and the Showgirl*) minded very much; Joshua Logan (*Bus Stop*) tolerated the coach; Billy Wilder (*Some Like It Hot*) , Howard Hawks (*Gentlemen Prefer Blondes*), and John

"You can't watch any other performer when she's playing a scene with somebody else." — Billy Wilder, director

Huston (*The Misfits*), didn't seem to mind at all. The ones who didn't mind made much better movies, vindicating Marilyn's judgment.

Montgomery Clift, recognized then and now as one of the finest actors of his time, co-starred with her in *The Misfits*: "She was an incredible person to act with ... she went over the fringe. Playing a scene with her, it was like an escalator. You'd do something and she'd catch it and it would go like that, just right up." John Huston added: "She went right down into her own personal experience for everything, reached down and pulled something out of herself that was unique and extraordinary. She had no techniques. It was all truth, it was only Marilyn. But it was Marilyn plus. She found things, found things about womankind in herself."

It is no wonder, then, that she was terrified. For someone with such a fragile identity to demand so much of herself, and not only to demand but to deliver — one begins to wonder less at her dread than at her courage.

Grudgingly, with both anger and admiration, Billy Wilder summed up any discussion of Marilyn Monroe's acting: "Anyone can remember lines, but it takes a real artist to come on the set and not know her lines and give the performance she did."

Earl Leaf's photos of Marilyn among her young fans and among her fellow stars were taken only minutes apart, but she's so much softer and more

*It's only reflected light, but Marilyn's mastery of make-up and costume creates
the illusion that she's shining all on her own*

natural among her fans. Her face is relaxed, her posture isn't tense, and

when she puts her arm around the boy she actually looks happy. Marilyn

smiled thousands of times for thousands of cameras, and her smiles con-

veyed many things, but it was rare that she looked genuinely happy.

When she's signing those autographs, that adoring girl is looking at her face, not her tits. Even the boy in uniform seems to be trying to read what she's writing, not looking down her dress. There was something in her appeal that neither critics nor studios were yet aware of — something you couldn't expect fans to articulate. That girl isn't staring with such joy at a sex symbol. It is hard to imagine the other sex symbols of that era (Ava Gardner, say) getting such a look, nor Marilyn's *How to Marry a Millionaire* co-stars, Lauren Bacall and Betty Grable. Such looks aren't given for stardom alone, and certainly not for sexual displays. Such joy is given in return for joy received.

An exchange was going on between Marilyn and America. Most of us were looking at her tits, yes, but what we were seeing wasn't quite what we expected — nor what we thought we wanted. Beginning with *Gentlemen Prefer Blondes* and *How to Marry a Millionaire*, we saw something else in her, some transportive quality that made many fans not only hunger for, but love, Marilyn Monroe. As though her very presence symbolized and made real something within our longing — our vague, never fulfilled, haunting longing for something that life seems to promise without giving, seems to *be* without being.

"I'm close, I can feel it, I can hear it, but it isn't really me," Marilyn would later say of her image, her aura. And so this longing, which is probably what human beings share most deeply, promises something

"Sometimes people start tailing me. I don't mind. I realize some people want to see if you're real." — Marilyn

close, that we can feel, we can hear, yet that never (or rarely) manages

to *be.* We loved Marilyn because she seemed a kind of evidence that our

longing wasn't for something imaginary — what we longed for could

take form and live.

"Marilyn Monroe was like a dream of Marilyn Monroe." — Lee Strasberg, acting teacher

So her death had more impact than the death of any other star, before or since — not because of Marilyn's tragedies but because of that girl's adoring eyes. Marilyn dead? A suicide? A murder victim? A promise had been broken. If Marilyn could die the way she died, our longing *was* imaginary. That, at any rate, seemed the verdict of her death — a verdict in which her dread connected with ours.

"Ah, I liked her so much. She was a nice lady. So witty." — Saul Bellow, novelist

The pressure that would drown her is well shown here as Marilyn is caged in by photographers and reporters

1956
A TOUCH OF GENIUS

"When the photographers come, it's like looking in a mirror. They think they arrange me to suit themselves, but I use them to put over myself. It's necessary in the movie business, but I often hate it. I never show it, though. It could ruin me. I'm not stupid."

— Marilyn Monroe

It's been six years since that afternoon in Johnny Hyde's backyard when Earl Leaf took his first photos of Marilyn Monroe, and not two and a half since the première of *How to Marry a Millionaire*. The woman at that première didn't look like the girl in the backyard, and this woman doesn't look like either of them. No matter how good a time she may or may not be having, she can't conceal the depths of her fatigue. Nor is she attempting (as she used to) to mask her intelligence.

This woman meeting the press in her living-room will be thirty in two months, yet in some shots she looks twenty, in others she could be

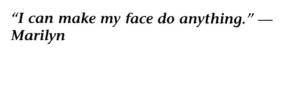

"I can make my face do anything." —
Marilyn

The only shot in which Marilyn reveals the "street" toughness she sometimes relied upon

pushing forty. She has entered a region (both within herself and towards the world) where categories like "old" and "young" are meaningless. Like Charlie Parker (thirty-four when he died) and Hank Williams (twenty-nine), Marilyn Monroe's presence bespeaks experiences beyond any normal measure of intensity or duration. The starlet of 1950 had to strain to give Earl Leaf poses. The super-star of 1956 has merely to be. She does no more than react to the people around her; what flows forth isn't pose after pose but woman after woman.

How many women are in these photographs? Some are so drastically different that if you place three together (see pp 78–9), you're looking at three separate people, or at least three drastically different aspects of a psyche. Yet these shots were taken within seconds of each other, in a socially superficial situation. It gives a hint at what it must have meant, at this time in Marilyn's life, to spend a day with her. Or a night.

She's at least as sensual as she ever was, but she's not forcing anything overtly sexual. She doesn't have to. It's in the air, radiating around her. But this is not the "baked Alaska" hit she used to project. This is a human, not an archetypal, sexuality — personal, immediate, specific to her. These are not photos of a sex symbol but of a profoundly sensual woman. The sex symbol was an expertly crafted artifact which you could receive on *your* terms — you could fasten to her any fantasy you liked; now the sex expressed in these photos has a

"She had this absolutely unerring touch with comedy." — *George Cukor, director*

woman attached, a complex and volatile woman with her own agenda, her own demands.

On this March afternoon in 1956, Marilyn hadn't had a movie out in nearly a year. That had been Billy Wilder's *The Seven Year Itch* (with the famous blown-skirt shot), a film in which the role Marilyn played didn't even have a name. In the credits she's just "The Girl Upstairs." Marilyn had broken away from the studios, then created her own production company; its first film, *Bus Stop*, would be released five months after this publicity session. So this was a session done specifically to keep Marilyn before the public during what would be her longest period between films. What she's showing America here is a far, far cry from *The Seven Year Itch*. The sex goddess of that film, or of Earl Leaf's last shots in 1953 — *she* looked as if she had no doubts about anything, least of all sex. Yet Marilyn could say: "A man who had kissed me once had said it was very possible I was a lesbian because I apparently had no response to males — meaning him. I didn't contradict him because I didn't know what I was."

It is hard, in the 1990s, to remember how shocking such a statement was during Marilyn's lifetime. Any hint of homosexuality was considered enough to ruin the biggest stars. Yet, almost as an aside, Marilyn confesses that at least in one period of her life she felt a fundamental sexual ambivalence — "I didn't know what I was." Both her male and female

Marilyn was the only cinema "sex symbol" adored by women as well as men

biographers have let it remain an aside. Doubtless it is only one of the many ambivalences that permeate Marilyn's presence on the afternoon of these sessions. For doesn't ambivalence color her mood here? Isn't it the very air of these shots? And since there is no more human quality than ambivalence, what shines here is Marilyn Monroe's humanity.

From our perspective, her change from goddess to human being seems obvious, but it was clearly lost on the studio heads and most of the press as well. Marilyn, using all her arts to express those changes, couldn't help but be baffled, and then frightened, that so few at the time really did see.

Does this look like a woman on whom the FBI had been keeping a file since 1955? (That file is still heavily censored for "security reasons.") Yes, in some shots she does. Does she look like a woman who, on hearing that Ella Fitzgerald had been barred from a Los Angeles nightclub, promised to sit at the front table every night if they'd book the singer? ("Marilyn was there," Ella later said, "front table, night after night... After that, I never had to play a small jazz club again.") Does she look like someone who sponsored the National Committee for a Sane Nuclear Policy? Possibly, possibly — for she looks both intelligent and unpredictable. Does she look as though she may already be addicted to pain-killers, downers and uppers? Or that she drinks too much? Or that the excruciation of her gynecological problems was

"When she's there she's there. All of her is there!" — *Clark Gable*

increasing every year? All of the above. There is something in that face that doesn't look healthy.

Does she look like a woman ready to risk everything, every single thing she's worked so hard for, to defend the man she loves? Later in 1956 Marilyn's lover and future husband, playwright Arthur Miller, was called before HUAC, the House Un-American Activities Committee. Anything leftist, even anything intellectual, was under suspicion in those years, and a censure from HUAC ended many careers, especially for people in theater and film. Associates begged Marilyn to stand apart from Miller till it all blew over. In her words: "Some of those bastards in Hollywood wanted me to drop Arthur, said it would ruin my career. They're born cowards and they want you to be like them."

Monroe accompanied Miller to the hearings and helped pay his lawyers' fees. It was an enormous public relations coup for Arthur Miller. Simone Signoret remembered: "One of two things could happen: her total destruction, or the rehabilitation in the eyes of the public of a man who, among others, was deprived of his passport; a man whose works were [at the time] neither played nor published." Because of Marilyn Monroe's popularity, the committee was never able to swell public sentiment against Arthur Miller, and eventually (again with her financial help) he beat HUAC in court. One can't imagine the goddess of 1953 in this scenario, but it doesn't seem improbable behavior

"I'm always running into people's unconscious." — Marilyn

for the sophisticated, world-weary woman in Earl Leaf's photographs of 1956.

Arthur Miller, by the way, was keenly aware of how much Marilyn Monroe could mean to him in the HUAC proceedings. When the committee asked Miller why he planned to visit England in the near future, thus hoping to stain him with hints of espionage, he answered, "To be with the woman who will then be my wife." Marilyn called her friend Norman Rosten: "Have you heard? He announced it before the whole world he was marrying Marilyn Monroe. Me! Can you believe it? You know, he never really asked me." The experienced playwright knew he'd upstaged the committee, and that the headlines wouldn't read MILLER A RED! but EGGHEAD TO WED GODDESS! Which is to say: even people who loved her (and there's no doubt Miller loved her) made drastic use of her image for their own purposes, and without asking.

Does she look, in these photos, like a woman who would lend herself to that? Very much so. There's a hunger here, and a vulnerability — a loneliness. Feeling as though she had little real life or identity of her own, it might be a comfort for her to adhere to the life-styles of others, at least for a time.

Even film directors who respected and liked Marilyn Monroe — John Huston and Billy Wilder, for instance — couldn't help sometimes speaking of

"If I'm going to be a symbol of something I'd rather have it sex than some other things we've got symbols of." — *Marilyn*

her with anger and frustration. Actually, it's a wonder any director spoke of her kindly. Her lateness and panics made their job hell. Directors who didn't like her showed no mercy. Laurence Olivier called her "a professional amateur." Otto Preminger said, "Directing her was like directing Lassie. You needed fourteen takes to get each one of them right."

Still-photographers had another view entirely — a view that corroborates the portrait of Marilyn as a woman with at least a touch of genius. Earl Theisen said, "Everything she does for a camera has been studied carefully. She knows exactly what she's doing. You can watch her, as you're focusing your camera on her, getting ready to turn it on. She knows exactly how far she wants to open her mouth, how much to raise her upper lip." A comment of Bert Stern's reveals how much she was in control of the process: "She'd move into an idea. I'd see it, quickly lock it in, click it."

Graham McCann summarized the difference: "The still photographers' response to Monroe, as a person, seems to have been directly opposite to that of her movie directors. Where the latter saw insecurity, inconsistency, and panic, the former were aroused to passionate awe..."

Earl Leaf did something valuable when he stepped back and shot the actual context of this session. How noisy that room must have been, and, with all these people and their flashbulbs, how claustrophobic. But in most of these photographs you could easily think that Marilyn was in

"I'd love to do scenes that the censors won't pass. After all, what are we here for, just to stand around and let it pass us by?" — *Marilyn*

"I guess I've always had too much fantasy to be only a housewife." —Marilyn

a room with no more than two or three others, and that moreover they were her friends.

"It's often just enough to be with someone," she once said. "I don't even need to touch them. Not even talk. A feeling passes between you both. You're not alone."

A feeling passes between you and her in these photos. As Graham McCann has written: "The person looking at stills of Monroe seems to hear her private voice, a sound which bestows a fine knowingness on her, a thorough command of the medium. She commands us from the still as she cannot from the screen." She also accompanies us from the still as she never did from the screen. (Only in *The Misfits* did the person on the screen bear a close resemblance to the person in stills such as these.) By "accompany" I mean: it is impossible to sense who the woman in *Gentlemen Prefer Blondes* or even *Bus Stop* may actually be outside her role; but a complex, utterly alive human being is vividly apparent here. Once you've seen her you cannot forget her.

"When the photographers come, it's like looking in a mirror." Someone who looked into mirrors as often as she did and, with her precise eye for appearance, must have watched herself change day by day, almost hour by hour, with a fascination mixed of deep fear and great expectation. Will the woman she's *trying to be* suddenly appear? Will it take another day, another year? Will it *ever* happen? I suspect that Mar-

"I don't mind living in a man's world as long as I can be a woman in it." — Marilyn

ilyn looked into mirrors with that level of anxiety all her life. And so her need to be photographed was profound. "It's like looking in a mirror." For Marilyn, the photograph was the mirror's report to her. Its judgment. Its confirmation. We feel great art in the photographed Marilyn, because art is greatest when it conveys the act of becoming. And that is all Marilyn did, most specifically in front of a camera: she became and became and became.

*"It was all truth, it was only Marilyn. But it was Marilyn plus. She found things —
found things about womankind in herself."* — *John Huston, director*

"Just as I had once fought to get into the movies and become an actress, I would now have to fight to become myself." — *Marilyn*

1958
THE DOWNTURN

"If I'm generally anything, I'm generally miserable."

— Marilyn Monroe

Something has broken. In the two years and four months since Earl Leaf's last photographs, there has been a shattering. In the photos of 1956, shot after shot reveals a sequence of many Marilyns. In the photos of 1958, *each shot* contains many Marilyns. There is a healthy way for that to happen, and a not so healthy way. A person can grow into embodying all their elements so completely that one feels a wholeness in their presence; or those elements can smash together at such a rate that instead of wholeness we're aware of a kind of flicker, as from a film projector, as various fragments pass across the face too quickly to catch. That is Marilyn's look now, and would continue to be until her death.

She is more touching than ever, and in many ways more beautiful than ever, but there's a delicacy about her that is new — as though she has less physical strength and less inner force. Her smile breaks your heart. She seems no longer quite of this world.

In the twenty-eight months since the last photographs, the love she put such hope in (and risked so much for) became first a marriage, then a disaster. The baby she wanted so desperately became a miscarriage. (Certainly not her first, though no one really knows how many miscarriages and abortions Marilyn Monroe had.) Then there was another suicide attempt, her first (that we know of) since Johnny Hyde's death. It almost worked. She was now a constant pill addict; in a condition of unrelieved, unbearable anxiety; and in almost continuous physical pain. Marilyn Monroe no longer had good days. Any activity took incredible effort. She lived in a state of breakdown.

The astonishing thing is that her two greatest film performances were still ahead of her. It makes one think of the last paintings of Van Gogh or the mid-Fifties recordings of Bud Powell. The marvel is that anyone living such a hell could work at all, much less work greatly. It speaks again of the strength of Marilyn Monroe's gifts. Something within this woman was uncannily resilient and determined.

"It was like kissing Hitler," Tony Curtis would say of his love scenes with Monroe. In *Some Like It Hot*, she would need often as many as thirty takes, sometimes forty, to get a scene right. After the first ten Curtis could feel his energy ebb, his focus smudge. Billy Wilder would testify that on the takes when Curtis was great, Marilyn was hardly there —

"It was like kissing Hitler." — Tony Curtis

she used the early takes to orient herself, even to learn her lines; by the time Marilyn had worked herself up to performance level, Curtis was spent. Wilder said he had to use Marilyn's takes every time, because when she's on the screen she's all you can look at. Curtis watched his performance evaporate on the screen, and hated her for it.

"I have never met anyone as utterly mean as Marilyn Monroe," Billy Wilder would say, "nor as utterly fabulous on the screen... She was trying to know a little more about mankind, but overlooking men under her nose. I

"Well, I think that's __his__ problem."
— Marilyn

would send the second assistant director, some decent kid, to her dressing room to inquire if she was ready to come onto the set and she would say, 'Why don't you go fuck yourself?' and slam the door in his face."

There are many such stories. Marilyn always had a temper, and something worse than a temper — a fury that could erupt unexpectedly, lashing out in any direction available, deserved or not. Now these outbursts, once sporadic, became part of her daily life. Fewer and fewer people on a set had anything good to say about her. Arthur Miller remembered Marilyn "slashing out to destroy. She didn't remember later the kind of fury she would project, and she would be sweet to the same person, like Billy Wilder for instance, and they would be puzzled and surprised."

It seems hardly real to us, because Marilyn never allowed that part of herself to be photographed.

That wasn't the only kind of lapse. Wilder recalled: "There was no rhyme or reason to her, total illogic. At one time, we were to go out to dinner and she came late wearing a fur coat, and she said, 'I forgot to put on my shoes. Can you help me? Can I borrow a pair?' And somebody went off to provide her with a pair of shoes.'

But Billy Wilder was pragmatic if he was anything: "I have an aunt in Vienna, also an actress. Her name, I think, is Mildred Lachenfarber. She always comes to the set on time. She knows her lines per-

"The luminosity of that face!" — Billy Wilder, director

fectly. She never gives anyone the slightest trouble. At the box office she is worth fourteen cents. Do you get my point?"

Yet it's this same Billy Wilder who, when speaking to biographer Fred Lawrence Guiles, relating one bitchy Marilyn incident after another, suddenly turned away, paced back and forth, and said with moist eyes: "We just happen to miss her like hell... Never a week passes when I don't wish she was still around... Because that whole category of films is lost. Her kind of genius is a lost art... Unless you have nerves of iron and total dedication, like climbing the Himalayas, let's turn back. But you go on with Marilyn, and it's worth it. The luminosity of that face!"

The legend of Marilyn Monroe, as it's commonly accepted, tells of a woman whose artistry went unappreciated in her time. Yet from *Gentleman Prefer Blondes* on, critics high and low praised her comic gifts. So did many of her directors, whether they liked Marilyn as a person or not. Wilder said, "She was an absolute genius as a comic actress, with an extraordinary sense of comic dialogue... Nobody else is in that orbit; everyone else is earthbound by comparison."

George Cukor, the director of *Let's Make Love* as well as of her unfinished film, said: "She was very sweet, but I had no real communication with her. You couldn't get at her. She was very concerned about a lot of rather pretentious things (she'd done a lot of shit-ass studying), and I'd

"Someone ought to go up and tell her she's Marilyn Monroe. She doesn't seem to realize it." — Albert Guestafeste, Marilyn's pianist

say, 'But Marilyn, you're so accomplished, you do things that are frightfully difficult to do.' She had this absolutely unerring touch with comedy. In real life she didn't seem funny, but she had this touch."

Just *who* failed to appreciate Marilyn Monroe's acting talent? The intellectuals who have, in a sense, codified Marilyn's legend — from Arthur Miller, Norman Mailer, and Gloria Steinem, to her lesser biographers — share a fault common to intellectuals: they undervalue comedy. Comedies almost never win the highest honors either from the Academy Awards or from the New York Circle of Film Critics (not to mention all the festivals), and the same is true of awards in theater and literature. In addition, literati of both sexes have decidedly sexist attitudes about clowns. Charles Chaplin, Buster Keaton, and Laurel and Hardy, are taken much more seriously than an auteur like Lucille Ball; Sid Caesar is lauded as though Imogene Coca's enormous contribution was somehow his creation; and comic geniuses like Mabel Normand and Judy Holliday become footnotes instead of legends. Beginning in 1956, when Marilyn moved to New York, that city's artistic elite welcomed her, took her in, treated her as she'd always wished to be treated — however mixed their motives sometimes were. So she found herself in the world of the New York literati, a world then still very much in the intellectual shadows of Freud and Marx — neither of whom was equipped to understand Marilyn Monroe. It was an intensely serious artistic community who, though

"I'm not interested in money. I just want to be wonderful." — *Marilyn*

they left us much, didn't leave us much laughter. Lee Strasberg's Actor's Studio was never known for its clowning. Under his tutelage (though against Arthur Miller's wishes), Marilyn began an intense regimen of Freudian analysis. It may be a good method for some people, but it seems to have shattered Marilyn's defenses while at the same time bringing her, and keeping her, face to face with her horrors. It is at this point in her life that she becomes afraid *all* the time.

Meanwhile everyone around Monroe — her husband, her guru, most of her other New York friends — held high the ideal of her being a *serious* actress, as though this was somehow more artistic than being a great clown. We cannot know what would have happened if Marilyn had found different mentors, people whom she respected, who had nothing to do with Hollywood, who loved and respected her for what she was, rather than what she might be. Her true genius and most natural gifts — being photographed and being a clown — found little reinforcement in the circles she'd chosen; and she wouldn't believe anything anyone from Hollywood told her. She needed people who could teach her to value what she was truly good at, and she never found them.

Never even looked, really. Rather, Marilyn accepted the standards of a severely limited vision of "serious," and devoted herself to those standards. Smashed herself upon those standards. Her last film, *The Misfits*, shot in 1959, is as fine an example of serious acting as you

"Marilyn played the best game with the worst hand of anybody I know." — Edward Wagenknecht, author

can find on the screen. But was she ready for it? Doing it broke her into more pieces than she could put back together.

Marilyn's look in these photographs of 1958 is very much the look of Roslyn in *The Misfits.* Written by her husband Arthur Miller as their marriage was falling apart, it was intended as both a portrait and a tribute. He admitted there were many lines in the script that Marilyn had actually said. He was writing a draft when she attempted to commit suicide, and there's been speculation that she couldn't bear that draft's revelations about her, and couldn't bear being used that way. Doubtless Miller didn't feel he was using her — we writers never do. Miller felt devoted to capturing, and helping her express on screen, her most indelible and ineffable qualities. But it finished their marriage. She couldn't trust him again. (As for Marilyn, she never said anything revealing, much less critical, of any ex-husband or lover. So Miller had violated not only her trust but her code.)

Yet Marilyn *did* perform *The Misfits* — in fact she gave it her best performance. And we know that it was virtually impossible to get Marilyn to do anything she didn't want to do. Still, we also know that there were times when she hated the script: "He could have written me anything, and he comes up with this. If that's what he thinks of me, well then, I'm not for him and he's not for me."

"See if I'm worth being a friend. That's up to you, and you figure it out after a while." — Marilyn

That comment indicates that she both assumed and expected a portrait from Miller. Her anger may have been that she, Marilyn, was so much smarter than Roslyn. Roslyn was a failed dancer; Marilyn was a gifted and successful actress, touched with genius. Roslyn had been beaten down by life; Marilyn was still a fierce competitor, fighting any way she could for as long as she could. Perhaps it comes down to this: Marilyn Monroe was better at what she did than was Arthur Miller at what he did. In the world of stars, she is one of the three or four brightest. In the world of playwrights, Miller wrote one great play, *The Death of a Salesman*, and then nothing that matched it. When HUAC attacked him, she had saved him; when she needed saving, he couldn't save her. Then, in her eyes, he couldn't even write her portrait. Her feeling of betrayal was total.

We inevitably associate Miller's Roslyn with photos of the last years of Marilyn's life. As magical as Roslyn is, when we do this we do Marilyn an injustice. Marilyn was both far more complex and much smarter. She felt that people failed to see the quality of her mind "because of the parts I play. If I play a stupid girl and ask a stupid question I've got to follow it through. What am I supposed to do — look intelligent?"

It may be that the tragedy of her life was that there wasn't anybody around to write a comedy as smart as Marilyn Monroe.

"She was a good talker. She spoke well on the national scene, the Hollywood scene, and on people who are good to know and people who ain't." — Carl Sandburg, poet

"It might be a kind of relief to be finished." — *Marilyn*

1962
FAREWELL, MY LOVELY

"If only they would be honest — just once."

— Marilyn Monroe

These photos are so strange. Taken shortly before her death, they show a haggard woman, her flesh pulled back on her face. The many selves that flickered through her presence only two years before — they seem to have departed. She looks hardly there. She still uses her skills to reflect more light than those around her, but she no longer registers on the camera with anything like her previous force. Only in the most shadowy shots does she look "herself," as though the shadows had already claimed her.

And who is the strange, small man accompanying her? She is thirty-six, and looks years older; he seems in his twenties. That would be nothing if they didn't look so incongruous together. It is easy (and certainly unfair) to see him as a kind of angel of death. But even if we didn't know that she was soon to die, we'd know that something is terribly wrong.

In these last Earl Leaf shots we see the woman who, three days before her death, went to a party and was asked to sign the guest register: though she had just bought her first home, under "Residence" she wrote, "Nowhere."

Since the making of *The Misfits* Monroe had moved from New York back to Los Angeles, leaving the world of the literati and entering another, darker world, a world of saloon-singers, gangsters, and politicians, who played by rules much harsher than Hollywood's — rules the literati could only imagine from a distance. Returning to L.A., Marilyn stayed briefly at a hotel, then moved into the Beverly Hills home of her friend Frank Sinatra. When she'd left Los Angeles five years before she was the hottest star in the world; now she was lost, and more than lost. Sinatra gathered friends of hers to cheer her up: Dean and Jeanne Martin, Clifton Webb, and others. And he bought her a little white poodle which she named "Maf" — short for "Mafia."

Apparently Sinatra also recommended the man who would be Monroe's last shrink, Dr Robert Greenson. Greenson had treated Sinatra a decade before. During the last weeks of her life she had a session with Greenson every day. It was Greenson's brother-in-law who would produce, or try to produce, *Something's Got to Give*, the film co-starring Dean Martin which Marilyn couldn't complete. When Marilyn got her own place again, her housekeeper, Mrs Murray, was recommended by Greenson. Greenson was in a unique position to monitor Marilyn's every move. It would be Greenson who called the police to report Marilyn's death, and Greenson whom they found standing by her bed. If the story of her suicide is a fabric of lies, they would be Greenson's lies. Frank Sinatra's "Rat Pack" adopted Marilyn Monroe like a mascot — Peter Lawford, Sammy Davis, Jr, Dean Martin, and their hangers-on. Through Sinatra and Lawford, she met Jack and Bobby Kennedy, and others in the Kennedy clan. Through Sinatra and Martin, she came into close contact with people who ran casinos for the Mafia, like Skinny D'Amato; and she came to the attention of, possibly even met, mobsters like Sam Giancana and Johnny Rosseli. I don't trace this web of connections from Dr Greenson to the Kennedys to Sam Giancana in order to imply any menace toward Marilyn from Frank Sinatra. In spite of all the stories of Sinatra's crudity, some of which are no doubt true, his singing and his best acting are records of a vulnerability, a tenderness, and a passion, that match Marilyn's own. There's every evidence that Sinatra, her sometime-lover, tried to be a caring friend. But it's clear that Marilyn Monroe's friendship with Sinatra was fateful for her. Through him she entered a world in which he and his circle maneuvered well, but from which she never returned.

J. Edgar Hoover had kept a file on Marilyn Monroe since 1955, so there's no way of knowing *who* had Marilyn under surveillance during her last year, but somebody did: in 1977 a workman repairing the roof of her last residence put his foot through rotted tiles and found the rusted remains of wiring and transmitters, estimated to be fifteen to twenty years old. Were they J. Edgar Hoover's? Sam Giancana's? Jimmy Hoffa's? All three? They all hated the Kennedys, and there has been reason to suspect their collusion on other issues, so why not this? For that matter, were the Kennedys taping her? As we shall see, she was more of a threat to them than to anyone.

In any case, we know that Marilyn feared she was under surveillance during her last months, and felt it necessary to make personal calls from pay-phones (when she wasn't too drugged to leave the house). At the time her fears were thought by friends and doctors to be a psychological symptom (or that's what they said). But later J. Edgar Hoover told the Kennedys about compromising tapes involving them and Monroe. Some sources claim Jimmy Hoffa also had tapes, which he planned to use against Robert Kennedy before RFK's assassination. With the discovery of the equipment, we at least know that "the Marilyn tapes" really existed.

And we know this: that however lost Marilyn Monroe was, she wasn't delusional. She was terrified, not crazy. She knew that her secrets could change the history of this country (for that matter, the history of the world). It's hard to imagine the strain this must have been for a person already so shattered.

"Don't give up the ship while we're sinking." — *Marilyn*

Her secrets, so far as we can prove, were simple and straightforward. No one doubts any longer the various convergent accounts of Marilyn's assignations with President Kennedy — how she would be summoned, fly to wherever he was, be whisked in and out in secret. ("I made his back feel better," she confided to a friend.) In that era, if their association had been proved he would have had to resign the presidency. (The Cuban Missile Crisis occurred only weeks after her death. How would it have gone if Lyndon Johnson had been President?)

But by all accounts she considered Jack Kennedy just a fling. It was Bobby Kennedy she fell in love with.

Her affair with Bobby (which may or may not have overlapped her affair with the President) was certainly common knowledge in the Kennedy family. Marilyn had met his sister, Jean Kennedy Smith, at a Sinatra performance at the Sands in Las Vegas. Now Smith wrote Marilyn saying, "You and Bobby are the new item!", and hoping that Marilyn would "come with him when he comes back East!" God knows what such approval could have meant to Marilyn in her fragile state of mind — especially when she found she was pregnant again.

Was it Bobby's baby? Jack's? Frank Sinatra's? Joe DiMaggio's? (DiMaggio was visiting her occasionally during this time.) Was it that man in Earl Leaf's photos? She was seeing several people. It seems she thought the baby was Bobby's, if only because he was the one she was in love with. That June — not long after she filmed the famous nude bathing scene; the same month in which she was fired from *Something's Got to Give* — she told photo-journalist George Barris:

"A woman must have to love a man with all her heart to have his child. I mean, especially when she's not married to him. And when a man leaves a woman when she tells him she's going to have his baby, when he doesn't marry her, that must hurt a woman very much, deep down inside." Within days of that statement, she spoke off-the-record with another journalist, W.J. Weatherby, saying of her current lover: "Only problem is, he's married right now. And he's famous, so we have to meet in secret... He's in politics... In Washington."

The last six weeks of her life were a vortex. On June 27, Bobby Kennedy was in Los Angeles, and several of Marilyn's biographers agree that they saw each other. On June 29, Sinatra headlined the opening of the new Cal-Neva casino — run by Skinny D'Amato, fronting for Sam Giancana. Marilyn came to the opening, and overdosed on pills and alcohol. In early July, she found her pregnancy was tubular, as her others had been. She had to have it aborted. She called Bobby Kennedy at the Justice Department several times that month, but he was no longer taking her calls. On July 27th, Dean Martin played the Cal-Neva and Marilyn was there again. Nick Tosches, in his brilliant biography *Dino*, describes the scene:

"... wandering around in a ghostly stupor, she spoke to Skinny D'Amato of things of which, as he told her, people ought not to speak. Dean knew what was wrong with her, beyond the pills, beyond the whole endless lost-little-girl thing: she just could not handle the dirty knowledge into which she had wandered, the black forest of Sam Giancana and Johnny Rosseli and her darling scumbag Kennedys, that world that lay past the dreamland... Dean knew things that people would not believe, things about the government sucking up to men such as Rosseli and Giancana, dealing with them in death, while others in government persecuted them; things about the black knights and the white knights fucking the same broads, drinking from the same bottle, and sharing the same spoils and murderous plots. Marilyn had glimpsed these things through her own errant innocence, and they had terrified her... Dean could see it: she was not long for this world. If she did not shut her mouth, she would not even need the pills to take her where she was going... [The next day] Monroe made her final call to [Kennedy's] office at the Justice Department. Less than six days later, on August 5, Monroe was found dead in her bedroom... 'There is more to what happened than anyone has told,' is all that Skinny D'Amato would say."

Marilyn's friend Robert Slatzer has said that she kept a diary of Robert Kennedy's "pillow talk," which included a CIA plot to assassinate Castro with Mafia hitmen. At least one biographer passes over

"I feel that beneath the facade of Marilyn there was only a frightened waitress in a diner." — Jack Paar, talk-show host

this, saying Marilyn wasn't disciplined enough to keep a diary at this point in her life, but it wouldn't have had to be a disciplined diary. A few scribbled pages would do to create the "time bomb," as Slatzer called it, in Marilyn's hands. Slatzer claims she told him that she was going to hold a press conference "blowing the affair wide open" unless Bobby Kennedy called her. Two days before the date she'd given him for the press conference, she died. According to another biographer, on her last night alive she phoned Peter Lawford and told him, "Say goodbye to the President." It's a matter of record that when Slatzer tried to publish this, his publisher was beaten and Slatzer's life was threatened. When ABC's *20/20* prepared a segment on this material, it was pulled at the last possible moment by news chief Roone Arledge, a friend of RFK's widow. Do these incidents mean Slatzer's material is the truth? No. But they indicate that some people were worried.

A profoundly unstable woman, the most famous woman of her time, capable of riveting world attention, and whose mere affair with the Kennedys would have been enough to bring them down, toppling the plans of God knows how many of the powerful ... a woman like this didn't need to have a diary or call a press conference to be a time bomb. She was already leaking her secrets to journalists, friends, and casino managers. And all the players had reason to believe she was being taped. It isn't such a leap to think that people like John Kennedy and Sam Giancana, who both had ordered other assassinations, might order hers — Kennedy, to protect the tremendous power he and his brother shared; the Mob, to keep Marilyn's secrets to themselves, on tape, to be used according to their own timing, not hers.

Powerful people, who saw and practiced murder as a tool of their professions, had powerful motives for murdering Marilyn Monroe. It's hard to believe that Jack and Bobby Kennedy, who treated women with such disdain and put such a premium on being "tough," would give up their life's ambition — give up the most powerful positions in the world — for someone whose suicide would be as easy to frame as Marilyn Monroe's.

As for Sam Giancana, he was murdered in the spring of 1975, when he had been subpoenaed to testify before a Senate investigation into an alleged CIA conspiracy to murder Fidel Castro in the early Sixties. Clearly, if the Mafia thought Marilyn knew about such things in 1962, as Slatzer claims, they would have had no hesitation in killing her.

Looked at this way, it's harder to believe that the Kennedys and/or Giancana *wouldn't* murder Marilyn Monroe. After all, it's likely that they were already working together to kill Castro.

When the police were finally called, on the morning of August 5, they found Marilyn's body in a "swan-like" pose, naked on the bed, her stiffened hand clutching a telephone. A stack of Frank Sinatra records was playing on the stereo.

They thought the scene strangely pristine. Tidy and clean. Suicides are usually messy. The bedroom door had been locked all night, said Mrs Murray — who, you'll remember, was Dr Greenspan's plant in Marilyn's home. But in the bathroom adjoining the bedroom, the water had been turned off for plumbing repairs the day before. This meant that Marilyn would have had to ingest a massive amount of pills dry. The only other way would have been to insert them by enema. But enemas are messy, and every surface in the apartment was clean. Yet Peter Lawford's wife at the time, Deborah Gould, has said he told her that night, "Marilyn took her last big enema." An ambulance service owner claims that Monroe, comatose, was taken a little after midnight to a hospital, where she died, and that then her body was returned to her apartment.

Mrs Murray now claims that Bobby Kennedy visited Marilyn that night, and that they argued. "Why, at my age, do I still have to cover this thing?" she says. Was his visit a last-ditch effort to get Monroe to shut up voluntarily? Patricia Newcomb, Marilyn's personal assistant, claims she doesn't remember that night, yet she nevertheless insists that Kennedy wasn't there; after Marilyn's death, Newcomb would be employed by the Kennedys. Bobby Kennedy was with friends when he received (official) news of Marilyn's death the next day. One of those friends, John Bates, later said that Kennedy took it "rather lightly... It was discussed in sort of an amusing way." A reaction that goes so far out of its way not to *be* a reaction, makes Mrs Murray's change of testimony more credible.

On the other hand ... Marilyn had just lost a baby. The two other failed pregnancies we know about were shattering to her. She died on the anniversary of her miscarriage of Arthur Miller's child — by all accounts, one of her worst experiences. People tend to remember such anniversaries. Her latest great love had been her most humiliating. Getting through any day was, quite literally, torture. Her intelligence was fogged, her body was ravaged and in constant pain. She'd attempted suicide twice before in her life, that we know of. Did she take *some* pills? Did the visiting Kennedy, or plants like Mrs Murray and Dr Greenson, see and report this, and did her murderers seize the opportunity? Or is the only mystery that, before calling the police, Murray, Greenson, and/or Marilyn's assistant Pat Newcomb merely cleared the apartment of any trace linking Marilyn with the Kennedys — and, in straightening out the apartment after their search, left it suspiciously clean? Still, that doesn't account for how Marilyn ingested so many pills with no water.

Hours before her death she called her dear friend Norman Rosten in New York, and made a plan to see him and his family in September when she came east. "We'll have a great time. We have to start living again, right?" It doesn't sound like someone minutes away from swal-

lowing handfuls of pills dry — though with a person as complex as Marilyn Monroe, you never know.

It is difficult to think of anyone more fragile, more haunted, than
Marilyn Monroe. A reductive explanation for her accomplishments,
the more or less standard psychological explanation, would hold that
her very stardom was the measure of her fragility — that she needed
to appear a goddess in order to conceal that fragility. Doubtless
there's some truth in that, but it leaves Marilyn (as so many analyses
leave her) as little more than a hysteric frantically compensating for
her hysteria.

What if, rather, she was a woman of uncommon intelligence, but
no education; a woman with no family, no supports, nowhere to run: a
restless, reckless woman, who couldn't settle for either Johnny Hyde's mil-
lions or obscurity; a woman driven by a need to express something, something felt urgently and wordlessly, as any artist feels it; a woman who had
taken the measure of her world and who found a way that she, in particular, could walk through it; a woman who knew only too well her own
cravings, terrors, hysterias, passions — knew only too well the odds
against her; yet who went on, into uncharted territory, wielding the only
thing in her existence that she could depend on: her beauty. Why isn't her
beauty, which she so painstakingly created, seen not as compensation or

victimization, but as an extraordinary act of courage — all the more courageous for the terrors that tore her without let-up?

For she could have withdrawn, even disappeared. She didn't have to look like Marilyn Monroe. People tell of days when she left her place without preparation, without make-up, without the carefully chosen clothes — and she would go unrecognized, even at parties.

She could have withdrawn, but she didn't. She insisted on *being* Marilyn Monroe, to the end. "I want the courage to be loyal to the face I've made." It became a horrific journey, but to reduce it to a symptom — symptomatic of her psychology, of the patriarchy, of whatever — robs Marilyn of her reason for being, and of her victory. For when it was all over, the images she'd taken such care to create didn't stop with her death, but took on their own life, grew in number and dimension, and have tattooed the psyches of everyone who has ever looked at her. That *was* what she wanted, even when she didn't want to want it. She paid a terrible price, but that is not uncommon when one wants such a terrible thing.

For isn't it a terrible thing, to be determined that everyone who sees you must remember you? Isn't that asking for a power over others beyond all proportion to the beauty she was prepared to give in exchange? Marilyn Monroe got the power she worked so hard for. Working stiffs and presidents, housewives and Queen Elizabeth, intellectuals and the secret police, paid her beauty their own kinds of homage. But getting power over them, riveting their attention, cost her power over herself. In the end she was crushed by what she'd set in motion.

After her death Sammy Davis, Jr, said: "Still she hangs like a bat in the heads of the men who knew her."

Hangs like a bat! It is a startling, macabre image, yet it's not so very far from a quality in her face caught by Earl Leaf's last photographs — shots in which she looks not unlike the transvestites who imitate her now.

"Goethe says a career is developed in public but talent is developed in silence," Marilyn commented. "It's true for the actor. To really say what's in my heart, I'd rather show than say. Even though I want people to understand, I'd much rather they understand on the screen."

Like anyone, she wanted life to meet her on her own terms. Like most, life met her instead on terms she had never imagined. Unlike most, she dared life again and again, sometimes intelligently and sometimes recklessly but always for the highest stakes, and she literally reshaped the world around her by the pure power of her luminosity — and by her brilliant way with a comic line.

If the Kennedys and the mobsters hadn't come into her life, it is hard to doubt that she would have lived longer. In her last interviews there is a resurgence of focus that didn't photograph: "As a person, my

"Half femme fatale and half child." — **Clifford Odets, playwright**

"Fame will go by and, so long, I've had you, fame." — *Marilyn*

work is important to me. My work is the only ground I've ever had to stand on. To put it bluntly, I seem to have a whole superstructure with no foundation. But I'm working on the foundation." This, and her last call to Norman Rosten, doesn't sound like someone with no chance left.

And if she had pulled herself together enough to work again (at her death she hadn't really acted in nearly two years); and if someone had written her an *intelligent* comedy? But all lives are full of such ifs. She might have made it, but she didn't. Her last year was a horror of humiliations, secrets, hopes, loves, terrors, overdoses, pain, pregnancy, abortion, an amazing modeling session with Bert Stern, magical footage of a swim in a pool, a dark small man on her arm ... a face that looked otherworldly even when well-lit, and bat-like when not ... a face that photographed like its old self only when blurred in the shadows ... some cogent words in a few interviews ... a stiffened hand (posed?) clutching a telephone ... a stack of Frank Sinatra records on the stereo...

Ten summers before, Twentieth Century Fox released her first co-starring role, the psychotic baby-sitter of *Don't Bother to Knock*. When, like Marilyn's mother and her grandmother, her character is led away as a lunatic to be locked up, Marilyn's last line is, "People who love each other..."

And that is all. It is a very Marilyn line, and has a very Marilyn way of hovering in the mind, inviting questions, paradoxes, one's whole life. It is a sentence that everyone begins and that no one ever gets to complete.

Dr Thomas Noguchi, the coroner who performed her autopsy (and "lost" much crucial evidence), made a startling statement in 1985. For the first time he admitted there were fresh bruises on Marilyn's body, bruises that "had never been fully explained." The interviewer asked, "Was Marilyn murdered?" Noguchi said, "could be." With those two words Noguchi admitted he had good reason to call for a homicide investigation – by implication, he admitted a cover-up. Add Mrs Murray's assertion, also decades after the fact, that Robert Kennedy visited Marilyn the night of her death and they'd argued. So a Marilyn bio-pic might end this way:

Close-up of Bobby's face, frustrated, frightened, determined. All the Kennedys' power may be wrecked by one statement from Marilyn to the press. Camera follows Marilyn, angry, face puffy with weeping and too much drink and too many pills. She doesn't know what to do, nor even where to step in her small house. She whispers, "People who love each other...." Close-up of Kennedy: he realizes nothing he can say will quieten her, and that nothing she can say will assure him of her silence. He turns suddenly and leaves. He goes to his car, but first he nods to a dark car parked down the street. He drives off. Two men get out of the other car and walk toward Marilyn's house. Close-up of Marilyn: her face can't quite cohere into a definite expression. Cut to the men outside. One knocks on her door. Close-up of Marilyn: she thinks it's Kennedy, she thinks he's come back. Her face brightens to a dazed, frayed exhilaration. Fade, not to black, but to a bright white screen on which our imaginations can project anything.

Or re-write the scene. Kennedy comes and goes, as Mrs Murray said. Marilyn, in a rage of despair, locks herself in her bedroom, pounds the walls, trips over her drunken feet, falls – creating the bruises. Then she pushes pill after pill down her throat. But before they take effect there's a strange change. She's finally done something definite about her unendurable situation. Soon all pain will end. Her face softens. There's nothing to worry about anymore. In the relief and release of that fact, Marilyn's eyes brighten. We fade, not to black, but again to that bright white screen, where anything can be projected.

Her luminosity itself is that screen upon which anything can be projected, anything can be imagined, anyone can claim her image for their own purposes, anyone can love or pity or dislike here, anyone can partake of her beauty, anyone can do anything but forget her.

"Someday I'd like to play Lady Macbeth." — Marilyn

1997
POSTSCRIPT

"I guess I look for freedom. Freedom from myself, even."

— Marilyn Monroe

With consummate craft Marilyn Monroe made herself unforgettable, and her image unavoidable; but like a magic spell in a fairy-tale, once this was done it could not be undone. To forget her horrors is to use her as merely the play-thing of our fantasies. But to remember *only* horrors, is to discount every image of joy that she left us. In this book alone there are so many! It is beyond human capacity to fake that much joy over such a long period of time.

Since all we have left are images, it may be all too easy to reduce her joy to an obsessive manic-depressive lust to be photographed. Yet Marilyn's intimates, while admitting her troubles, have each repeated some version of Arthur Miller's statement: "Being with her people want not to die." Which is to say that in her presence people often felt exactly what we feel from her photographs. Marilyn may have been doomed, but Marilyn was for real.

June 1, 1997, marks what would have been her 71st birthday. Had she lived, would she have been a fat old drunk and pill-pusher, a pathetic denial of all we cherish in her photographs? Would psychiatry's new drugs have brought her a measure of calm? Would she be known

"You said one day that life subsists by its own inner contrasts. If that's true, I'm the most alive person in the world!" — Marilyn to writer Hans Lembourn

primarily for exposing the Kennedys' peccadilloes and machinations, thus bringing them down before their assassinations, so they too would have lived? Or would her resiliency have won out, and as she aged would she have become (as she once planned) a superb character actress? She guided women of her generation toward her vision of beauty; would she have guided them, by her brave example, through the inevitable dissolution of beauty?

Remember: she wanted to grow old without face-lifts. She said, "Sometimes I think it would be easier to avoid old age, to die young, but then you'd never complete your life, would you? You'd never wholly know yourself." If she had survived the terrible complications of her life in 1962, would she have set a public example of a woman growing into old age fiercely trying to know herself? And can't you see a Marilyn buoyed by the feminist liberation movement that picked up steam only five years after her death? Can't you see Marilyn revelling in the early militant stages of that movement, and being one of its most public warriors?

"Anything's possible, almost," Marilyn said. She meant that, and she lived it. And, because she did, all we can say for certain is that, if she'd survived, any of these scenarios would have been possible. *That* is her real epitaph: that no one, anywhere, ever, can write the final word on Marilyn Monroe.

"You've got to get the most out of the moment. Let's make some mischief."
— Marilyn

*How shall we remember her? Perhaps Earl Leaf always recalled
that first session in May 1950*